WHAT DO YOU WANT TO BE WHEN "YOU" GROW UP?

A Guide for Adults Beginning a Second Career

by

Yvonne Starks

authorHOUSE®

AuthorHouse™
1663 Liberty Drive, Suite 200
Bloomington, IN 47403
www.authorhouse.com
Phone: 1-800-839-8640

First published by AuthorHouse   5/13/2008

ISBN: 978-1-4343-7259-8 (sc)

Library of Congress Control Number: 2008903472

Printed in the United States of America
Bloomington, Indiana

This book is printed on acid-free paper.

DEDICATION

I dedicate this book to my two children, Keisha and Desmond.

To Keisha, for growing up to be the wonderful woman that she is and for supporting me in writing this book. She was there for me every step of the way, reading, and coaching me, and I thank her for that.

To my teenage son, Desmond, for putting up with the late dinners and his computer time (since I was busy putting my thoughts on paper and time just slipped away). He was there to listen as I read passages from this book, and he gave me feedback on what he thought, and I thank him for that.

I thank God for both of my children, whom I love more than life itself. They have strengthened and encouraged me throughout the years in more ways than they will ever know, and I pray that their lives will continue to be enriching, satisfying, and fulfilling.

Acknowledgements

I want to thank God for giving me the strength, courage, willpower, and foresight to write this book. Without him guiding, leading, and many times carrying me in this life, none of this would have been possible. He makes a way out of no way. If the words he has given me to put into print help at least one person, then it was all worthwhile. When prayers go up, blessings come down!

To my friends with whom I shared the writing of this book and for their encouraging and inspiring words. Thank you Faith, Bert, & Eddie!

AUTHOR'S NOTE

A list of website resources are listed in this book that may be useful in your research and planning. In no way am I affiliated nor have any connection with the companies that sponsor these websites and furthermore, I disclaim responsibility for any adverse effects arising from the use of these resources.

CONTENTS

What Do You Want to Be When "You" Grow Up?

CHAPTER ONE

ALL GROWN UP

We've all asked our children this question: "What do you want to be when you grow up?" We've all heard all types of answers to that question. Most of the time our adult children end up with careers far different than what they thought they wanted as children. However, there may come a time in your adult life when you find yourself, at fifty, fifty-five, or sixty years old in a dead-end job or your company has gone through a downsizing and you were laid off. Perhaps you've just grown tired of what you're doing and want to change your life and what you're doing with it.

You might be in a position to take an "early" retirement from your job, and you begin to think…what do I do now? In this day and time, there is no such thing as "retirement." Even if you retire from your job, most likely you will find yourself still working to make ends meet. Social Security benefits do not begin until age sixty-two; however, this is not your full benefit. Therefore, if you are drawing your benefits at age sixty-two, you are getting less than what you would receive at a later age. This will probably not be enough for you to live on unless you have made highly profitable investments in your earlier years to afford you a nice income in your later years or have been the beneficiary of a sizeable inheritance. This is not the case for most of us; therefore, we have to continue to earn an income. The Social Security Administration has probably already started to send you an annual document informing you of your benefits when you retire at a certain age. If you have not begun to receive these, you may request them from your local Social Security office. This will give you an idea of what you can draw as a monthly benefit when you retire, depending on your age at the time.

We're all aware of the rising cost of healthcare coverage, and it's going to get worse before it gets better. You may need to continue to work to pay for your healthcare plan if you are one of the fortunate ones who still has a retirement healthcare package from your employer. Medicare doesn't begin until age sixty-five (unless you are disabled), and it doesn't cover everything. Therefore, you will need a supplemental plan to cover the expenses that Medicare doesn't cover in full. In addition, you must pay Part B under Medicare, which covers doctors' expenses. This amount increases each year and is deducted from your Social Security payments each month.

Now, with this in mind, what are you going to do for your second career? Have you thought about what you want to be when "you" grow up? This question is very different than what a child may think he or she wants to do. A child knows this is not a decision they have to make now. It's so far in the future that they don't really have to give it a second thought. It's based solely on what someone in their family is doing or a sports figure they admire or someone they see on TV or hear on the radio. For someone our age, it's a decision that we are faced with now. We don't have years to think or fantasize about it. Therefore, we must decide what we want to do for the rest of our lives or at least until our second retirement. There may be something you've always wanted to do but didn't have the resources or time to put into. Or there may be something you've always wanted to do but thought you were incapable of doing. As we get older and realize that time is shorter than we used to think, we begin to put things into perspective. We realize that we have to make the time to do some of those things, and with modern technology, such as computers, the resources are at our fingertips…literally!

Once we become a certain age, we also realize that what we used to think we were incapable of doing we now know that we are capable of… we were just scared to step out there and try it.

Maybe the word "scared" is not correct. For many of us, when we were younger, we had children to rear and would not think of quitting our jobs to try something not considered to be the "norm" for fear of failure. Of course, if we failed, what would become of our children? How would we take care of them—especially if you were a single "mom" or "dad" and the only parent the children had to depend on? Now that the children are raised and supporting their own families, it's time to put those fears to rest. The "fear" of failure is still there somewhat, but not at the intensity it once was, because if you fail now, it only affects you and not the entire family. What's the phrase? "There's nothing to fear but fear itself." Basically, when you think about it, it's just the fear of the unknown. You will never know if you can be successful until you try it.

Okay. Now that you've made the decision to change your life, how are you going to change it? What is that second career? Is it real estate, consulting, opening a daycare? You have to decide what your passion is and make it work for you. It's okay to discuss this with your friends and family, and they may have suggestions for you, but the bottom line is you have to find your niche…what makes you happy. It may hit you like a ton of bricks one day, or you may only have to put into motion an idea that's been in the back of your mind for some time. However you discover it, don't procrastinate. Find out what it takes to make it happen. Whether it's pounding the pavement, reading, surfing the Internet, etc., you should put your wheels into motion. Networking is also a good resource. While casually talking with friends, an idea may come to you. You may see a need for a certain market that can help others that will give you self-gratification as well as earning an income.

Earlier in your career, you may have been working just to put food on the table and to provide a shelter. It may not have been the job of choice, but nonetheless you felt blessed to have a job when there were so many people who didn't. Now it's time to take that leap and do what you really want to do. You may need to consider a job that provides benefits if that is a concern. If that is a need, consider working for a company rather than being an entrepreneur. If you do not have retirement healthcare from your previous job, be sure to check out companies that offer a retirement health plan in the event that you retire from that company. Many companies no longer offer a health plan after retirement, so be aware of their benefit policies before you accept the offer. If benefits after retirement are not a concern, research positions that offer what you are looking for in salary as well as fulfillment. If your passion is to be an entrepreneur, do your research. Tap into resources that can aid you in obtaining a small-business loan, choosing the right location, etc. Be careful not to stretch yourself too thin. You don't want to end up in a place where your emotional well-being is not being satisfied. You'll end up back where you started.

It's all about deciding what your "American Dream" is and going for it. This will take conscientious planning and a strong desire to reach your goal; however, it is attainable. You must change the dialogue with yourself from *can't* to *can* and become a more positive thinker. Positive thinking along with positive human action results in positive reality.

Now let's forge ahead and prepare yourself for the next phase of your life.

CHAPTER TWO

A FEELING OF NERVOUSNESS

Are you feeling a sense of anxiety? It's entirely normal to be apprehensive about making a major change in your life. Step back and take a deep breath. Take two or three deep breaths, because you are about to do something to change your life for the better. Doubt may be swirling in your head, as well as a feeling of discomfort. Allow yourself a little bit of time to go through this, because we are only human and you should take the necessary steps to process these emotions. However, don't dwell on it too long. The longer you concentrate on the doubt, the more likely you are not to take the forward steps to living your dream. You're having these feelings because you are getting ready to step outside the "box." Most of your life, you have probably done things that are comfortable for you or that you have just fallen into without really having a choice in the matter. Isn't it wonderful that, at this time in your life, you can finally choose your course?

Now you're about to live your dream, and it's time to be excited! Put all of those negative feelings where they belong...in the "box" that you're stepping out of, and leave them there. It's time to think positively as you begin your new journey. You will not be able to enjoy your new endeavor if you're operating on a negative level. Your insecurities will hold you back. You can do whatever you set your mind to do as long as you are prepared. Preparation is not only the physical part of it, but the mental aspect as well. If you start down this path thinking, "I can't do this," or, "This is a mistake," you will probably not succeed. You must grasp and hold onto your positive inner strength that is the driving force of intervention.

It's time to stop talking and start doing. What many people don't realize when they begin something other than what they are familiar with is that it is the start that stops you. We tend to focus more on what it takes to begin something rather than the outcome. Once you take that first step, it becomes a little easier. By the time you take that fourth or fifth step, you'll realize that there is a life beyond what you were doing before. I know this is all easier said than done, but you will and can get through it. You are bound to have a degree of uncertainty, but it's time to release the tension that has you all pent up inside. It's important to acknowledge the feelings you're having, deal with them, and then put them away. There's no room for negativity on the road you are traveling. Negative thoughts can, if you let them, eat away at you like a cancer. That's why you have to arm yourself with positive thoughts to drive those negative forces away.

Get rid of those inhibitions that have kept you stagnant throughout the years. They have no place in your life now. It's a new day and a new beginning. Give yourself permission to be all that you can be. Let go of what you were yesterday and embrace new possibilities. It's time to start thinking about what you want and need out of life. Self-care is essential in moving towards your goal. You will not be considered selfish by taking care of yourself, because you must help yourself in order to help others. We all have a tendency to get so caught up in everyday life taking care of our responsibilities that we forget to take care of ourselves along the way.

You must believe in yourself and your capabilities. Step out of that comfort zone you are accustomed to and take a chance. Yes, it may be considered risky; however, there are certain risks in life that you must take in order to fulfill your dreams and desires. There's no better time than now to do it. Don't put it off any longer, because there may come a day, fifteen or twenty years from now, when you look back over your life and wish you had done this or that and feel that now it's too late. Don't allow this to happen to you. Apply your skills, talent, and energy into whatever you want to do today, because tomorrow is not promised.

Don't allow yourself to get caught up in that "prison of self-doubt." If you continue to doubt yourself and your capabilities, you will become trapped and eventually convince yourself that you cannot make this happen. Once this occurs, it will be difficult to bring yourself back on track. I said difficult, but not impossible. It doesn't matter what someone told us we were or were not throughout our lives. You do not have to be shackled to your past or what once was. You need only to have the willingness to bring about this change.

Once you have calmed down and processed your feelings of anxiety you will be able to take pleasure and pride in what you're getting ready to accomplish. You will be able to focus on the quality of life and all that it means to you. Look forward to the future with self-confidence because your future is on the rise. You have the courage and the potential to succeed as long as you remain positive. So, step out of that "box," put your fears aside, and live your dream. You can do it and you're worth it!

CHAPTER THREE

DON'T GIVE UP

Now that you have decided what you want to do and have begun the journey, you may start questioning whether you're doing the right thing. Follow your instincts and your gut feeling. If it doesn't feel right, then maybe this isn't what you are destined to do. Remember, this should be something you are passionate about. Passion does not mean drudgery. This should be an exciting time in your life, and you should have fun doing it. Everyone is not cut from the same cloth; therefore, you may not enjoy doing what your best friend has found success in. Do what makes you feel good inside. Don't compare yourself to anyone else, because you are unique. God did not make any two people alike.

It's helpful to have a support system in your endeavors, but don't be discouraged if someone in your family doesn't totally support you in what you are doing. They may not be where you are in this particular time in your life and may not understand why and what you are doing, and that's okay. Talk to them and let them know that this is something you have to do for yourself. No one can live your life for you but you! Accept constructive criticism, but don't confuse it with someone attempting to dampen your spirit or make you second-guess yourself. There are all types of people in the world, and some will be there for you and some will not. Do not allow anyone to interfere with what you feel is right for you. On the other hand, if you have people in your life who do support you, share your thoughts with them. They may suggest an idea that you hadn't thought of, or they may be instrumental in putting you in touch with someone else who can assist you.

While going through this, you may need someone to lean on or bounce ideas off of, or perhaps just someone to listen to you when you're feeling a little down or discouraged. I highly recommend that you confide in this person your innermost feelings. Allow yourself to be open with the people who are supportive of you and accept any assistance they may offer you. Don't feel that you have to go through this alone. You may be surprised at how willing others are to help you if you let them. Keeping these feelings bottled up inside will prevent you from moving forward with an open mind. Share those feelings of inadequacy, and once they are out, you will feel better and it will allow you to function at your full capacity. There will be times when you feel that you just can't make the journey. Having someone to listen to you, encourage you, and have faith in you is sometimes just the boost you need.

Always remember that you have the power to make things happen. The path to higher goals in life may not be smooth and you may endure a setback, but don't let this slow you down to the point where you want to give up. You may be confident one moment and frustrated the next; however, any goal worth achieving will require work. Nothing will be handed to you on a silver platter. Focus on your inner strength and your self-knowledge. You haven't lived this long and not been faced with challenges. Even though this may be something you haven't considered before in your life, it doesn't mean you can't do it. Think about other challenges you've had and how you overcame them. You didn't just throw in the towel and say, "Forget it." You applied the knowledge you had and prayed. You may have sought advice from a professional, and you got through it.

The going may be slow at first as you lay out your plans, but don't despair. It is better not to rush into anything as meaningful as what you are beginning to embark upon. Take your time and be sure you have all your ducks in a row, especially if you're going into business for yourself. Rushing into this could leave you disappointed should you not succeed because you didn't take the time to think things through and research all avenues. A well-thought-out plan is always the best plan.

Whatever your challenge may be, put your best into it and know that you are doing this for you. Motivate yourself by repeating, "I can do this." You have the capacity to do what you set your mind to do. Don't let obstacles get in the way of your dream. When obstacles arise, work through them and get beyond them. Don't use them as an excuse to give up. Instead, think of them as stepping stones towards your future. Don't try to move the mountain; just go around it. There is a quote that I heard once, "Surviving and living your life successfully requires courage. The goals and dreams you're seeking require courage and risk-taking. Learn from the turtle. It only makes progress when it sticks out its neck."

As you delve into this process deeper, you will find that inner strength I've been talking about and may be pleasantly surprised at the outcome. You may be able to go places further than your wildest dream. There's no other feeling like being happy and pleased with yourself with the knowledge that you have accomplished your goal. As Dr. Phil would say, "When you know better, you do better."

CHAPTER FOUR

WORKING FOR A COMPANY

If you have decided to pursue your ideal position within a company, do your homework! First, check out the company's history. How long have they been in business? What is their financial status? What is the company's forecast for the next two years? You can find all of this information and more on their web site. You may also want to check the stock market for several weeks to gain knowledge about their stock margins. You will want to know their benefit policy...health, dental, vision, PTO, medical leave, 401k, and vacation, etc. Last, but certainly not least, you will need to know the salary for the position. Is it what you're looking for? Even though this may be your "dream" job, consider whether or not your earnings will satisfy your current financial situation. You want to be happy, but not robbing Peter to pay Paul every month!

Once you've done all of this and it meets your qualifications, you need to prepare a resume. You can go to the library or the Internet to learn how to do this. If you do not own a computer or laptop, it would be wise to invest in one at this time. You will be amazed at the information that can be found online. It may have been years since you've prepared a resume or you may not have ever prepared one. In any event, you need to prepare one that is precise and will sell yourself to the company to whom you are applying. A good resume should consist of one page plus a cover letter. The cover letter should state the qualifications and experience that you can bring to the company as well as your attributes. It should be no more than two or three paragraphs at the most. You don't want the recruiter or whoever is reading it to become bored before they get to the actual resume. At the top of your resume, you should include your name, address, daytime phone number, and e-mail address. (This is another reason why you will need a computer.)

There are several designs you could use that will provide you with different layouts. You then want to list your education. If you do not have a college degree or have not taken any college courses, then list where you attended and graduated from high school. Be sure to list any classes you have taken and any certificates you may have earned. Listing your hobbies and interests is optional. If your hobbies or interests will be directly related to the position you are applying for, then it would be a good idea to list them. If not, then it's okay to omit. Next, list your work experience, with the most current first. List your job responsibilities tailored to the position for which you are applying. For example, if you recently worked in retail and you are applying for a childcare position, you will want to list your communication skills as well as your skills in paying attention to detail.

Refrain from using phrases like, "I was the best at," or, "My manager praised me." You don't want to sound egotistical or full of yourself. Your references will speak for your character and your qualities. If you worked twenty years at your last job, only list the job you held before the latest. Most employers are not interested in anything you did more than twenty years ago and haven't done since. If you've held several jobs within the past twenty to twenty-five years, then it's appropriate to list the last several positions you've held. Be careful not to go back too far. A good thing to keep in mind is that employers are more interested in what you've done within the last ten to fifteen years.

You can provide names and numbers of references, preferably someone you have worked with. Friends are good references; however, they cannot speak of your work ethic, and that is what an employer is looking for. They want to know what kind of an employee you are. Depending on the relationship you had with your former manager, you may or may not want them to contact him or her for a reference. If you prefer for them not to contact your former manager, then tell them. If you are currently working and would rather your present company not be aware that you are pursuing other ventures outside the company, then it's okay for you to inform the company that you are interviewing with that you do not want them to contact your present manager. Most companies are understanding of this and will not question you. Of course, this is not information that you would list on your resume; this is something you would discuss face to face with your interviewer. If you prefer not to list references on your resume, you could state that references can be obtained upon request.

It is probably not a good idea to list a salary request. Many times salaries are negotiable, and that will surface during the interview process. If you feel you must state something about salary on your resume, you could note that salary is negotiable. Once your resume is complete and you are satisfied with it, have someone who is knowledgeable regarding resumes critique it for you. Since this is new to you, they may have suggestions on how to shorten or lengthen it or to project other affirmations about you that you may not have thought of.

Submit your resume to several companies that you are interested in. Many companies prefer that you submit your resume via e-mail rather than snail mail. If you are submitting via snail mail, be sure to choose a good paper stock to print your resume on. Presentation is important. Since some companies prefer to reply via e-mail rather than phone, you will need to constantly check your e-mail account for replies. Once a company that wants to schedule an interview has notified you, make sure you know the exact location of the company. The last thing you want to do is to show up late because you couldn't locate them. Ask them about parking and which entrance to enter for the interview.

If you've heard from more than one company within a week, be sure not to schedule your interviews on the same day. There's a possibility the interviewer may be so impressed with you that they may want you to interview with someone else within the company in the same day. If you've scheduled another interview that day, you may not be available to stay for the second interview. This could cost you the job; therefore, do not schedule more than one per day. You want to remain flexible, because that could be what that particular company is looking for.

Now that the interview is scheduled, you'll want to consider your wardrobe. Dress to impress, but don't overdo it! A nice business skirt suit or pantsuit for women or business suit for men is appropriate. Ladies, don't go overboard with the jewelry. Large gaudy earrings or necklaces are a no-no! Keep it simple and business-like and wear low-heeled pumps or flats. There may be a lot more walking involved than you anticipate and you don't want to concentrate on how bad your feet are hurting while you're trying to sell yourself! Also, be aware of your cologne. That scent that your husband or wife is so crazy about may be too powerful when you're enclosed in a small office.

Try not to be nervous. To put yourself at ease, try a mock interview at home with family prior to the "real" thing. Have them ask you a few questions that you think an employer might ask and respond to them in a professional manner. Bear in mind that an employer will ask you questions that your family didn't; however, this process will help prepare you. Be prepared to discuss what kind of person you are...your characteristics, how you function under pressure, etc. They may ask how you would handle a particular situation on the job. It's okay to think before you speak. Don't blurt out the first thing that comes to mind. It's better to take a few moments to think of the right answer than to be concerned that you're taking too long thinking about it and respond too quickly, thereby giving an "off the wall" response. Employers expect you to be somewhat nervous; however, focus on being yourself. Portraying someone that you're not will surely surface and would be misleading if you were to be hired by them. Also, remember to make eye contact. This is very important when you are speaking to someone, not only while you are interviewing, but in everyday life. This indicates that you have nothing to hide and you have self-assurance.

You may be struggling with the fact that you're not as young as you used to be and that a future employer may not be interested in you because of your age. Let's face it....there are some employers who would rather have a younger workforce. Then again, there are many that prefer a more mature individual. Experience and wisdom go a long way and are definitely selling points to a prospective employer. The mature generation tends to be a more loyal employee. Maybe this is because we've been there, done that, and have learned that dependable and reliable employees are a viable and critical need to a company's business. Don't try to hide your age. Be proud of your maturity and the lessons you have learned. Age is only a state of mind.

CHAPTER FIVE

ENTREPRENEURSHIP

If you've decided that you want to be an entrepreneur, you will need to prepare a business plan. You can get assistance with this on the Internet or at the library. It would be advisable to have an attorney review it because you want to make sure all the legal aspects are met. Next, you will need to find out how to gain financial backing. Like many of us, you are probably not financially able to start your own business with funds of your own. That's why you will need to research how you can obtain the money you need to get started. Attend workshops in your area that will afford you knowledge about starting a business. Were you aware that you could get government grants to begin a business? Grants do not have to be paid back…this is free money!

You may not receive enough from a grant to run your business; therefore, you may need to obtain a small-business loan. Take time to comparison shop. This is a big adventure; therefore, you want to invest a lot of time in choosing the best loan with as little interest as possible. Check out many financial institutions and banks. If you are a member of a credit union, see what they have to offer. Compare the APR (annual percentage rate) from all institutions and read the fine print. Many people have signed contracts that are legally binding and did not read the fine print and found themselves in a lot of unnecessary debt. There again, have an attorney review your documents before signing anything! Beware of get-rich-quick schemes. If someone advises you to invest in something with a large return within a short period of time, it's probably not a good idea. If it sounds too good to be true, then it probably isn't. If it were that easy, then everyone would be doing it and making millions!

You need to be certain you have the qualifications needed to start your business. Let's say, for example, that you want to open a daycare. If you have not worked with children before (other than your own), you should attend childcare classes to become a licensed daycare provider. There are programs available that do not require years of training that you can attend. Arm yourself with as many certificates as you can in childcare, including a first-aid class. Parents want to know that you have the skills and knowledge that it takes to run a daycare. Put yourself in their place...would you want to leave your child with someone who does not have the credentials to take care of your child eight hours plus a day?

Once you have finished your training and earned your degree, certificates, and license, you will need to find a location. Keep in mind that it would be advisable to choose a location that's on a bus route. This would be convenient for parents who rely on public transportation. You want to make sure your location is easily accessible and that you have ample parking for your parents dropping their children off. Therefore, you don't want to choose a location that's on a busy street where it is not convenient to turn into your establishment or to get out of due to traffic. However, you don't want to get too far off the beaten path either.

Check out the neighborhood! You don't want to open a daycare in a neighborhood where there is undesirable traffic…and I'm not speaking of vehicles! You can visit your local police station to find out if there have been numerous police calls in the area. You will also want to inquire if there is a registered sex offender living in the area. This is public knowledge. If someone has a prior conviction of being a sex offender and has now been released, they must register their address with the city in which they are living. Talk to neighbors to gain information about the neighborhood as well. If you find anything that is demoralizing, stay away from the area! You want the children in your care to be safe, and parents will not want their child in a neighborhood that isn't safe and secure.

You will need to decide if you want to lease the facility or purchase it. Depending on the location, you could purchase a house and renovate it to suit your daycare needs. Many daycare centers began as a renovated house, and as the business expanded, a new location was sought to accommodate the growing business. You will also need to gather information on the cost involved for cribs, mattresses, tables and chairs for "little" people, suitable toys for inside and outside, sleeping mats, books, games, etc. Again, refer to the Internet for ideas on what supplies you will need and visit other daycare facilities.

You will need to hire personnel, such as a cook as well as a staff to take care of the children. States require that you have a particular teacher/child ratio. Therefore, you must hire a certain amount of employees per children as required by your state. You won't be able to direct, cook, and look after the children by yourself. Familiarize yourself with food programs in your state that are offered to licensed daycares. You may not be aware of this, but you cannot feed the children breakfasts, lunches, and snacks using the same menu you would use for your own family. Guidelines and menus must be followed per the food programs.

In order to decide on a fee schedule, you could visit other daycares to find out what they are charging. Your fees would be different according to the age of the child. For example, you would charge more for infants than you would for toddlers simply based on the care an infant would require compared to a toddler. Your state may have programs available that assist parents in paying their daycare expenses depending on their income status. Tap into all resources. There are probably a lot more programs available than you are aware of, and it's in your best interest to be knowledgeable and to obtain the facts about all of them.

You should think about activities for the children. Children of all ages must be occupied and their minds stimulated; therefore, you will want to purchase games, toys, books, crayons, paper, etc., for the appropriate ages of the children you are caring for. Be sure to choose educational books, toys, and DVDs. Parents will be pleased to know that their child is actually learning while they are in your care and that you are not just babysitting.

Perhaps you want to invest in real estate by buying and renting houses or flipping them. In order to get started, you should contact a real estate agency. They can provide you with a listing of homes in your price range. It might be advisable to purchase a house that is in foreclosure since these houses are generally owned by banks and can be purchased at lower prices than other houses. Banks want to rid themselves of these houses because they have been seized from homeowners who could no longer afford them. Therefore, the prices for these houses are typically negotiable. The money you save can be used for repairs.

Even though you will not be living in this house, you should still consider the neighborhood and whether or not it's in a good school location and a low-crime-rate area. Renters and buyers with families often make their decision on a house based on the school district; therefore, it's imperative that you keep this in mind when you are making your purchase. In addition, you need to make certain that the house is in a location that is accessible to grocery stores and other shopping facilities. You want to be sure the area is attractive to prospective renters or buyers.

Once you've decided on a house to purchase, consider how much is needed to make repairs in order to get it ready for rent or resell. Make sure your loan will be enough to cover these expenses. Be sure to have the house inspected by a certified inspector. This normally takes place after a purchase agreement has been made; however, if serious problems are discovered, you might be permitted to withdraw the contract. There are some states that allow an inspection prior to an agreement. You should check with your realtor to find out what the law is in your state. It is in your best interest to have this inspection done. You don't want to purchase a house and find out later that a lot more repairs are needed than you originally thought. This is not an investment where you want to have surprises. A surprise leak in the roof could cost you thousands! After you have your inspection and know what kind of repairs will have to be made, you then need to decide what work you can do yourself as opposed to hiring someone to do. Even though you will save money on doing most of the work yourself, do not attempt any repairs such as electrical or plumbing if you are not skilled in this area. Leave this type of work to qualified individuals if this is not your area of expertise.

After you have considered the cost of repairs and decided that this is the house you want to purchase, make an offer. As I stated previously, a foreclosed house would be a wise choice if you are purchasing for rental property or to resell, depending on the condition of the house. If your offer is accepted and once you have closed on the house, it's time to start making your repairs. Try to get as much done as you can within a timely manner, since time is money. The longer it takes for you to rent or resell, the more money out of your pocket with no return. You will need to decide if you are going to rent to families with pets. You should consider this when determining your security/cleaning deposit fee. After all, cats and dogs generally do some damage to carpets and yards; therefore, you should have a substantial security deposit to cover any costs involved to clean the carpet or repair landscaping if your tenants vacate the premises.

When establishing what you will charge for rent, do some research in comparing what other homes comparable to yours are going for. Keep in mind that not all renters are "good" renters and you may run into some that will try to "skip" out on you. There is no hard fast rule to follow with being a good landlord, other than to always be fair without being a "pushover." You will have to be firm when necessary and stick to your renters' agreement. Make sure your renters understand everything in the agreement prior to them signing it, and if they do not abide by it, follow the consequences you have listed in the agreement. One way to motivate renters to be "good" renters is to have a good relationship with them and keep up with repairs as needed. Just like you don't want them to hide from you when it's time to pay the rent, don't hide from them when repairs are needed. Try to put back extra money each month if at all possible to handle those unexpected repairs as well as money for property taxes and insurance.

If you purchased a house with the intention of flipping it, keep all of the above in mind when you are purchasing...such as a good location, good schools, low-crime-rate area, etc. All of this will be helpful in your resell. Put the house on the market as soon as possible after you have made your repairs. There again, time is money. Consider the cost of comparable homes in the area as well as the money you have put into the home for repairs when you set your selling price. Selling the house yourself (by owner) instead of going through a real estate agency could save you money since you won't have to pay the realtor cost; however, you should also keep in mind that you will have to do everything that a realtor would normally do. This would include, among other things, acquiring an appraisal, certified inspector, title research, and making arrangements for the closing.

Being a real estate investor requires careful planning and research or you could drain yourself financially...especially if you get in over your head. Don't overbuy. Start out with one house; see how that goes before you purchase another one. Hire reputable people to help you with this as well as attending workshops, researching information on the Internet, etc., to make certain you understand all of your options. This can be a lucrative business for you if you are equipped with the necessary information and knowledge and have done your research.

There is a lot more planning and information gathering you will need to do before you open your daycare or purchase your investment property; however, I have just pointed out a few of the things you will need to think about in order to get started.

A good rule of thumb is to remember to research whatever your vision is before you put it into practice. You can never obtain too much information!

Chapter Six

Engaged

Webster's definition of the word "engaged" is a promise or pledge. You are now engaged in this process and should put your best foot forward. You should enter this promise to yourself with all that you have and more. You have taken the necessary steps to get where you are, and you feel complete. You have a feeling of self-worth and have connected with your inner strength. You are happy and ready to set the world on fire. This sounds a little like a "love affair," doesn't it? Well, in a sense, it is a love affair with yourself and your accomplishments. It's okay to be "in love" with what you are doing. The feelings you are experiencing have progressed from being in love with the idea of it to actually being in love with what you are doing. Wrap your arms around it and embrace it. This is the beginning of a beautiful relationship. However, like any other relationship, it must be nurtured in order for it to grow. Just because you have worked hard to get where you are doesn't mean that you can slack off now. You must continue to feed this relationship in order to sustain it.

You must "buy in" to this concept in order for this to be effective. You can't just say, "I'm committed," and let it go at that. Continue to do your research and whatever it takes to make this relationship flourish. There is a direct correlation between the commitment and the goal. If you are not honest with yourself and your heart is not in it, you will not reach your goal. This is why it's important to be sure that this is *your* vision and not someone else's. If this is something that your heart desires, you will reap the raptures and you will be inclined to do whatever it takes to make it work. So give it your all, and your enthusiasm will promote a long-lasting relationship.

Look at this engagement process as being a probationary period you are going through before you are actually a member. While on probation you have the right to rethink the entire process. This is a little resting period before you actually make the final commitment. Of course this period should not be used to open up that "box" and bring forth all of those old negative feelings again. It's just a little breathing room to collect your thoughts. Don't convolute things by rehashing the past or having a "panic attack."

There will be conflicts along the way, but you can combat them with the tools that you now possess. When a glitch surfaces, face it head on, apply what you have learned, and get through it. Like with anything in life, nothing is going to be a bed of roses all of the time, and life is a challenge, but what makes the difference is how you perceive and handle it. In the past, you may have had a whatever attitude. Now, you know it's not "whatever"; it's "however." When life hands you lemons, what are you going to do with them? You're going to make lemonade!

You have a new outlook on life and have gained confidence in yourself. Your whole thought process is different than what it used to be. This is a monumental feat in your life and should not be taken lightly by you or anyone else. Stay on course and don't allow yourself to veer off the track. Keep yourself in the race, because you have come too far to turn back now. Your personal growth is beginning to materialize, and you are now a recipient of greater things to come. You are broadening your horizons, and you're ready to be optimistic instead of pessimistic. Your glass is half full instead of half empty. You are expanding your parameters and realize that you no longer have to or need to live within that little "box." There is going to be an explosion in your life, but you're ready for it because you're prepared… mentally and physically.

You will become fully engaged in this process as time goes on. This pledge you have made to yourself is a solemn promise that you can keep.

Don't be afraid of it, because the outcome will bring you great joy. Just remember to stay true to your commitment and continue to believe in yourself. Believing in oneself is a true test of self-confidence and perseverance. Even when the going gets tough, you have to hang in there because you have a purpose and a goal. Sacrifices will have to be made in this commitment not unlike any other commitment you make in life. It may be in the form of time, energy, or a financial sacrifice. Whatever it requires, be prepared to handle it head on. You have learned that adversity will strike, and hopefully you are now equipped with what it takes to overcome it.

Once you begin to see positive results from your efforts, you will realize that achieving your goal was not nearly as hard as you first imagined. Becoming self-engaged will bring to the surface all the wonderful qualities you possess. That beacon in your life will keep you moving in the right direction. You have established your own path, and your reward will be both gratifying and fulfilling.

Chapter Seven

Displaying Creativity

If you are working for a company you should suggest ideas to make your job satisfying and meaningful as well as convenient. When that lightbulb flashes, explore that idea and turn it into a reality. An idea is just an idea if it remains in your head. Manifest your thoughts and concepts. Employers are grateful to have employees who challenge themselves. Who knows…you may suggest an idea to your company that reduces their expenses, and you could be rewarded monetarily or otherwise. You will also feel a sense of pride in knowing that the company adopted an idea of yours.

Don't be afraid to make a suggestion for fear that someone else may have already thought of it. Maybe they did or maybe they didn't. You'll never know until you suggest it. There have been people who have had an idea and kept it to themselves, thinking that it may sound foolish, and someone else came along and made the same suggestion and was compensated for it. Remember the saying that there is no dumb question? There is also no dumb suggestion. The suggestion of the simplest of things could turn into something huge. Remember the people who came up with the idea of liquid paper, post-it notes, etc.? Those individuals are now millionaires.

If you are an entrepreneur, be creative with your business advertisements. Advertise your business through signage, newspapers, radio, etc. There are newspapers that will allow you to advertise your business free of charge if you are a new entrepreneur to the area. Investigate all advertising possibilities. You want to get your name and business out there for the public to see. Create flyers to distribute throughout the neighborhood. Don't forget about family and friends to help you advertise your business. Provide them with flyers to post at their job sites along with business cards. The more you advertise, the better.

Another idea is to have a suggestion box at your place of business for your customers. Once per month, choose a suggestion to put into practice. For the customer who submitted it, give them a discount or something free of charge from your business. You'll be surprised how this will "catch on" and you will attract more customers. Remember, all it takes is for one person to tell another and that person tells someone else and so on. You can't always anticipate what your customers or clients want, so ask them and provide it to your clientele. That's the key to a successful business: supply and demand. A happy and satisfied customer will tell their friends and family, and that's how you gain exposure.

There are many ways to express creativity. You could have a "grand opening" with discounts offered to the first ten or fifteen customers, depending on the size of your business. Develop a catchy phrase to print on your business cards that flows with your establishment. Customers will associate the phrase with your business, and this will set you apart from other like businesses. Think, think, think, and let your creative juices flow.

Manage your business in a manner that is appealing to others. Decorate your facility during the holidays. Keep your displays neat and attractive and clutter free. Remember to place mats at your doors during inclement weather. This is for safety reasons if you have tile floors or to maintain a clean carpet. Your establishment's floors should always be kept clean and free of debris. Customers enjoy walking into an establishment that has a clean, upbeat, and captivating atmosphere. Depending on the type of establishment, you might want to have soothing music playing in the background. When you create an ambience that is pleasing to the soul, it could uplift one's spirit, therefore changing their mood. A customer could walk in having experienced a very trying day on their job and not in a very good disposition. If you have created an atmosphere in your establishment that is pleasant and relaxing, they could walk out with a 180-degree change in their mood.

Stand behind your product and your business. One of the worst things you could do is to not allow a return of a defective item. If a customer returns an item that is defective, either exchange it for the same or similar item or give them a refund. Consumers are turned off by businesses that are not accommodating in this manner. This is a sure way to promote bad publicity. You want their experience at your establishment to be a positive one where they will want to return. Happy customers are your ultimate goal.

CHAPTER EIGHT

A CHANGE OF SEASON

Your family and friends may notice a change in you. You may not have realized that your unhappiness was apparent, because you thought you were doing a good job of concealing it. It's amazing what others can see about us that we think they can't. There are many people who can see beyond the surface of our personas. Sometimes we are so busy portraying ourselves as a certain kind of person that we lose our real self along the way. After years of doing this, it becomes habit, and when we finally face our true self, we may have to be introduced! Our true selves have been hidden for so long that we don't even recognize ourselves.

People may say you have changed or that you are a different person. You are not a different person; you're just a person who thinks differently. You have merely developed the side of yourself that has always been there but was trapped for many years. You have inner peace now that you're enjoying life to the fullest. You have finally realized and come to terms with your vocation. You may be wondering why it took you so long to realize this dream that you used to think was so far-fetched. Just remember that there is a time and a season for everything.

Do not consider the past as time wasted, because you have to go through life's challenges in order to bring about a change. Life experience is a wonderful teacher. As life students, we have to live and learn as we go. What life teaches us cannot be read in a book, taught in a classroom, or told to us by someone else. We have to experience it in order to gain knowledge. The knowledge that we pick up along the way is useful in our future.

We learn all the tricks of the trade, so to speak. If we didn't go through these things, we would all be like baby birds that cannot fly…just flapping away but not gaining any stride.

When there is a seasonal change, the temperature changes. Your temperature will change too as you move into your season. You may not remain the same even-tempered, "come what may" person you were before. You may show a lot of excitement and have a higher energy level than before. You may exhibit behavior (in a good way) that is not familiar to your friends and family. You may become more assertive whereas previously you may have been considered passive. You are more comfortable when making decisions because you are allowing yourself to embrace your talents and gifts and you are surer of yourself. What was pleasing to you before may no longer be pleasing or acceptable. All of these changes are coming to pass because you are no longer depriving yourself of life's possibilities.

You may need to get used to this person who now thinks differently. When you think differently, you are bound to act differently. You may have a new gait to your step or make a change in your personal appearance such as your hairstyle or hair color. These changes are a direct result of you stepping out of your "box." Go ahead and make those changes if that makes you happy. It's okay to pamper yourself. There is nothing wrong with change as long as it's in a positive manner. Changes in our lives are good for us and keeps us focused and balanced. So go ahead and indulge yourself; you deserve it!

Discovering who we really are is almost like being reborn. We may have gone through most of our lives identifying ourselves with what we do rather than who we are. This has caused us to lose sight of who we truly are. Now that the mask has been removed and self-awareness has set in, we and others can see positive results. Self-awareness is a powerful thing. You realize now that you are not a victim of circumstances but rather a victor of better things to come. It's all a matter of how you look at life. Positive thinking brings about positive results, just like negative thinking brings about negative results. It's as simple and complex as that!

There are some people who have negative personalities and never change throughout their whole lives no matter what. They never have a good thing to say about anything or anyone. Being in the company of someone like this is depressing, and you wonder how they can go through life being negative all the time. A person like this is not a happy person, and they have become so caught up in their own little world that they have lost sight of what life is all about. If this fits the description of someone you know, try to reach out to them...let them read this book. Anyone can change if they want to. All it takes is the willpower and the courage to make it happen.

Just like the four seasons of the universe, people go through life seasons. Now I'm not saying that you will go through four different seasons. Typically, people go through two seasons in life. The first season is from childhood through midlife. This takes you through the "growing-up" years. The second season is from midlife through their senior years. This takes you from the "growing-up" years to where you are today… all grown up! I just want to make you aware that it's completely normal to change during this process and don't want you to think there's anything wrong with you as you're experiencing this change. Make those positive changes as you go through your season. Be proud of yourself and the person you have become. Your family and friends will be proud of you as well. This is your season in life!

Chapter Nine

Determination Prevails

A little determination goes a long way. Granted, it may have been somewhat of a struggle, but you have recognized your abilities and taken personal responsibility for your life. Knowing that your goals were within your reach and grabbing the opportunities along the way helped you to gain the stamina you needed to move forward. You have proven that you have what it takes. It hasn't been easy, but it's been worth it. There will still be good times and bad times; however, with your determination you can handle whatever comes your way.

Don't even entertain the thought that you will "crash and burn." The unknown no longer intimidates you because you now have the strength to conquer whatever is presented to you. You know that there are alternatives, and you're no longer afraid to investigate what they are. When you change your attitude, you are more open to receive opportunities that are available to you. Living with a closed mind doesn't allow you to grow. Those same opportunities have always been there, but you couldn't see them, either because you were not ready at the time or because you were shy about seizing them.

Consider yourself fortunate that you are now able to not only recognize the possibilities but to actually foresee that long-awaited dream. You just needed that jump-start to get you moving in the right direction. Listen to your heart as you are traveling down this road. You may want to turn left because it looks like a smoother path, but your heart tells you to turn right. You question that turn because the path may look to have a lot of bumps and potholes; however, you take it because you are determined to make it down the road, come what may. It's clear to you that the right turn is a little more complicated to maneuver, but you learn a few things along the way that would not have surfaced had you taken the left turn. That's why we have to be determined to reach our goal even though the road may be bumpy.

It's a privilege to be able to ascertain your capabilities and put your skills and talents to work for you. There was probably a point in your life where you thought none of this was possible or probable. Now you have found that it's all a matter of cause and effect. What causes you to do something will have an effect on your life. Once you make up your mind, you can see it through to the end to enjoy a more fulfilling and meaningful life. The single most important factor to remember is that your newfound determination will take you where you need to go.

The upside of determination is success and how you define it. Is it defined by how much money you make? Is it defined by your educational status? Is it defined by how expansive your home is? Or is it defined by how happy you are with yourself, how peaceful your life is, and how kind you are to others? Money does not denote happiness. There are many wealthy people who are not happy. I know many educated people who are not happy. There are people who live in very large homes in nice neighborhoods who are not happy. So, as you can see, having *things* does not make people happy no matter how successful they are in life. I would be willing to bet that most people would trade in all of the above if they could be guaranteed success in life in the form of peace, love, and the pursuit of happiness.

Recognizing your dream and going after what you want is one of the most important decisions you have ever made in your life. Pursue it with zest and valor and the conclusion will be two-fold. Take a fresh look at where you are in life and where you are going. Following your dream and where it will take you will require dedication and determination on your part; however, if this is your calling, you should not pass up the opportunity. There are some of us who have been privy to golden opportunities in life and just allowed them to pass us by. Don't miss out on this chance to take your life in a new direction.

You're at the top of your game, and at our age, we have a wealth of experience. Now just put all that experience and knowledge to work for you. Most of us have more skills and talents than we think we have. It's an awakening once we uncover this vast knowledge and realize our potential. This is the most opportune time in your life to explore your aspirations. Exercise your right to cultivate your dream and make it come true. You can be transformed by a dream.

CHAPTER TEN

LIFE CHOICES...
GOOD, BAD, & UGLY

Reflect back on where you were just a short time ago. Isn't it amazing how far you've come? Now that you've applied that inner strength that I've been talking about throughout this book, it's a wonder and a joy what you have become. The best thing about all of this is that you made a conscious decision to make this change. You stepped outside the "box" and made it happen! You pulled yourself up by the "bootstraps" and made this terrific change in your life. This wasn't just a midlife crisis but a midlife dream come true.

Peace and happiness are two of the most beautiful sentiments in life. It's sad for anyone to go through their entire life without experiencing either. The beauty of it all is that it doesn't take that much to have it. A little encouragement, a dose of willpower, some determination, and a whole lot of prayer will get you there. People sometimes get in a rut because they are doing the same thing year after year. It becomes humdrum after a while and they think, "That's life." But you and I know that it doesn't have to be "just life." You can change the course by just making up your mind to do it. It's easy to just stroll through life letting things happen. It takes work on your part to make things happen for the betterment of your well-being.

It's all about making choices. Sometimes we make bad choices when we think they are good for us. We later come to realize that the grass is not always greener on the other side or that what may be good to us is not always good for us. Therefore, that "good" choice we thought we made turned out to be a "bad" choice after all. Some of the bad choices we make are based on what frame of mind we are in at the time. We may be depressed or saddened by an event that has occurred in our lives; therefore, we make rash decisions instead of taking the time to allow ourselves to heal and then using good judgment to arrive at a decision. Some choices are made because of the encouragement of others when that choice may be a good one for them but not for us.

Then there are those "ugly" choices we make in life. These are the ones that we look back on and say, "What was I thinking?" Even though this may have been a bad patch in our lives, it helped strengthen us and hopefully made us less vulnerable to those type choices. Even if you have made an ugly choice, it doesn't define who you really are. Learn from the experience and make the choice not to repeat it. You don't have to continue to live with that decision. Remember the phrase, "You've made your bed; now you have to lie in it"? Well, that's not totally true. You don't have to live with bad or ugly choices. You may have to endure a period of disdainfulness for a while until you are able to make a better choice, but don't let this govern who or what you are. We as humans make mistakes. None of us are perfect, and you shouldn't beat yourself up over it. We do have a responsibility to strive for perfection, however, we should not condemn ourselves when we blunder. We don't have to live with a mistake or bad choice for the rest of our lives.

When it comes to life choices, we should not make these on a whim. Many times this is what gets us into trouble. We sometimes tend to be impulse choice makers. It's okay to sometimes be impulsive with insignificant decisions, but we need to use more discretion when it comes to a life choice. Take, for example, the decision you have just made to change your life. You probably didn't just wake up one day and decide that you were unhappy with the current situation. It may have just occurred to you that you could do something about it, but that feeling of restlessness has been building up for months or possibly years. This took time for you to come to this realization, and it will also take time for you to make a decision of sound judgment about the course of action you are taking.

Now that you have made it through the hurdle, encourage others who may be in this situation. However, make sure that your own house is in order before you try to tell someone else how to run his or hers. Remember that in order to help others, we have to help ourselves. It's difficult for others to take us seriously if we're trying to encourage them to change their lives when our own lives are in turmoil. Once you have your life in order and are living your dream, you should share your knowledge about how to get there with others. When they take a look at what you've done and how you did it, they are more apt to try it themselves. You will be a testimony that dreams do come true.

We are only on this planet for a short period of time, and we all deserve to be happy and content.

True, there will be pitfalls along the way, but that only makes us stronger. When we struggle and go through bad times and survive, it makes us appreciate life all the more. Life is a journey with ups and downs, highs and lows, triumphs and failures. How we react to these facts of life is what makes all the difference. You can choose to wallow in self-pity or you can choose to weather the storm, apply what you have learned, and move on to a brighter and better future knowing that there is light at the end of the tunnel.

You have the ability to make any choice in life you desire. The kind of choice you make is up to you!

Resources

www.socialsecurity.gov

www.medicare.gov

www.aarp.com

www.preparingaresume.com

www.businessplans.com

www.governmentgrants.com

www.rentalagreements.com

About the Author

Yvonne Starks is a first time author and resides in the Midwest section of the country. She is a divorced mother of two and enjoys helping others. She was employed with a major electronics firm for many years until her retirement and decided to write a book about searching or realizing your "passion" after retirement. Her book is based on research as well as her personal life experiences. Her goal in writing this book is to enlighten, broaden one's self image, and hopefully aid others who may be in this situation and may not know how or what to do to make this life changing event materialize.

www.ingramcontent.com/pod-product-compliance
Lightning Source LLC
Chambersburg PA
CBHW022118170526
45157CB00004B/1686